The Peach Tree

ANN SPIER

outskirts press

CONFESSIONS

IN THE MUSEUM

DEAD PEOPLE

EDEN

HOPE

THE PEACH TREE

My every fiber recalls
summer wafting late and low
in the garden near the garage.
I taste the tart and tangy radishes
I'd rinsed clean in my mouth,
crisp, from the radish row.

Even the fuzzy musty touch of it
was erotic, pulsed and puckered
as pleasure will do, before lips and heart
catch up to the dewiness of desire and destiny.

I ate the peach right off the branch,
the sweetness dribbling down my dress.
Soon to be scolded, but no, never mind
the pain of the switch brought to bear
on my barely-haired legs.
Stubborn, I wouldn't shed a tear.

The indignity came later.
Acid, the allergist alleged,
in tomatoes, citrus, and stone fruit,
one must be careful not to eat too much.
All the good things one must not touch.
So many pitfalls in this land called life.

CONFESSIONS

THE MONSTER UNDER THE BED

The monster slashed and slandered,
switched and scratched
screamed and swaggered,
then left in a lurch.
The monster hurts
when it lurks and harms
in spite of open arms.

The monster bleeds in a pool
with queries about helmets
and architectural school.
The monster aches
for approval
and hopes for love
beyond reason.

The monster is wounded
and won't strike for now.
She needs your touch.
Is forgiving too much?

SITTING

It isn't so much the thoughts,
some good, some cringe-worthy,

unlike the memory of trees,
of mountains, of forests and streams,

cliffs, valleys, an evening breeze,
clean air to breathe.

Can life get even slower?
I am in awe of the goodness

of nature that begets the goodness
of God, so I sit

and wait for more.

WHAT YOU SEE IS WHAT YOU GET

The Quakers meant well
when they said goodbye.
The malice, the complaints,
and judgement deserved
were always reserved, never given.

What you see is what you get,
they said.

So I carry their expectations,
unspoken, yet understood,
to act with integrity,
honesty, kindness and truth,
but I can never meet their bar.
I've already failed so far,
in countless ways, yet I must try,
and try again to merit their praise,
if indeed, there is praise in what they say.

What you see is what you get.

A PAIR OF GLASSES

I lost one and broke two.
What is it I'm not seeing?

Am I the speck in your eye?
Or the log in my own?

IT'S A GOOD THING YOU WROTE IT DOWN

I have to write it down these days.
If I remember now, it's gone
by the time I step away.
I say to myself "I'll never forget",
and then I do, into the kitchen I go.
What for? I don't know
until I've reached the office.
Was I going to get a snack, perhaps?
I look foolish as I stop and stare.
The facts flee, I must declare
my mind is bare.

JOB

Sometimes I feel like Job
You know the Bible guy?
He got the worst of it,
without knowing why.

I am crabby, I am cranky,
I despise the world and everything in it.
It's hateful, no other way to spin it.

Scabies, scoliosis, self-inflicted exile,
self-centered piety, and self-endowed bankruptcy,
Remembering with regret,
ruing a past, never to forget.
Self-sabotaged screw-ups,
chances missed and mocked.
Schizophrenia, the worst diagnosis,
ruled and conquered all.

I am crabby, I am cranky,
I despise the world and everything in it.
I am hateful, no other way to spin it.

Sometimes I feel like Job.
You know the Bible guy?
He got the worst of it,
without knowing why.

Oh silly fellow! Don't you know as long
as a single blade of green grass grows
there is hope?

THE OLD CRONE

There once was an old crone.
She liked to be alone.
Certain habits all her own
supported and sustained day by day.

She did one thing at a time,
even if it was just to sleep,
No matter the dream,
the sleep was not that deep.

She drank and ate whatever,
a long life not her concern.
Why care what others think?
No bra, no makeup – who gives a dern?

She talked to trees as she passed by.
They need our love, she mused.
Every bloom along the way
was worth a moment's stay.

A smile and a compliment she paid to all,
no matter how ugly the blouse.
It may be the only light of a long, dark day,
the stranger may become a friend.

She walked with dogs,
feasting on a fluffy sunrise.
No detail of a show-off nature
ever escaped her eyes.

She used library books in hard copy,
having no use for technology.
"The old ways are good enough," she said,
"ample for my physiology.

Everything changes anyway.
Just to be, enough for today.
I don't need the ruckus
nor whatever else transpires."

The feast of life has settled on her wrinkled
systems of many years and she carries
the after taste on her tongue.
She will shed no bitter tears.

She accepts all with equanimity,
anticipating the dessert to come.
"Let it go" is her mantra and
living is adequate indeed.

There once was an old crone,
who liked to be alone.

SITTING REDO

I am fundamentally a lazy person.
My favorite activity is sitting.

I used to be strong, worked all day long,
kept going when others said enough,
my energy bunny, brave and strong.

Then I learned to listen to my inner ear.
The world that speaks to me there
is still and silent and I cannot bear to leave.

I must be a witness to the here and now
that transforms and uses me.

I am fundamentally a lazy person.
My favorite activity is sitting.

I AM BLESSED WITH A BIG TUMMY

It runs in my family, this monster mine.
I've heard complaints for years.
My grandmother, mother, and sister, of course,
cursed equally in every clime.

Once, at breakfast in the college cafeteria,
with new students from a southern school,
"When's the baby due?" she asked. An unforgivable guffaw,
since we'd met the night before, both girdled and gridded

for inter-sexual war, "What baby?" I squawked,
incredulous of her cruelty. She was embarrassed,
but the virginal abdomen already protruded
when I was only 120 pounds and 20 years new.

So let's present the case for our gullets.
Humongous hidden closet for a Thanksgiving feast,
or All You Can Eat at the Red Lobster buffet.
An all-purpose receptacle, convenient for any occasion.

Sitting zazen, a fine sense of balance,
plus a comfort to babies and dogs, a prop
for a cuppa or heavy books, its strength limited
only by the elasticity of a pair of jeans.

But how awkward would it be
if nothing below those pendulous breasts
supported the diaphragm's safety wall
for a little thing that required a hug?

And finally, consider this: If it weren't for the forward
leaning profile of your enormous tummy,
it would be your nose's fate to protrude,
to lead your fat self into the future.

WE'RE ALL THE SAME

I am scarred.
I've done bad things, I have
rues and regrets, bad bets and debts,
and the sting of love betrayed.
I am scarred.
Are you?

I am scared.
I am scared I'll run out of money.
I am scared the earth cannot sustain us
and Russia will rule in Ukraine.
I am scared of cancer and pain.
Are you?

Scarred and scared.
We are flawed –
everyone of us.
Yet there is joy to choose.
There is love to choose.
There is hope to choose.

We are all scarred and scared
and sacred.

THE HORNET'S NEST

My mind is all a-jumble,
Unruly wisps stick out and others curl
within and beneath and the knot
at the top scarcely holds.

My barrett is an inadequate jailor
that would prevent their escape,
their voices a dissent showing
unwilling participation in this caper.

The mirror presents a mess indeed, but
I know what lies beneath is even messier.
the One-ing I so desire evades me.
The hornet's nest broadcasts

my confusion, my failure
to listen, to feel, to see
to understand I must cede
my borders to be with You.

A DOG KNOWS THE NOW

What if we could learn to live as the dog lives,
waiting and hoping for what comes next?
Food? Treat? Walk?
Dancing with anticipation and joy,

walking shoes on, leash clipped in elation,
shivering in expectation,
yipping with jubilation,
the best part of every day.

It's the dog's privilege to serve, to watch,
to take this trip to see all is well.
What if we could live as the dog lives,
Knowing the now?

THE MOCKINGBIRD

The mockingbird knows me as we walk along,
pulling the dogs on a leash.
I laugh and sing in imitation, a poor one indeed,
but he knows I am calling the best I can,
asking for his beautiful tunes,
for the trills and titillations of his masterful repertoire.

He sings for my pleasure, I know it, and mine alone.
He knows I need to steal a tune or two,
to borrow from his melodies. He knows I am bereft
just now of my own pitiful song. So I smile and
lay down my angst for a few holy moments
to enjoy a conversation with my talented friend.

A SLAB OF SALMON ON A CEDAR PLANK

Is anything so perfect?
Butter, some herbs, a teeny splash of salt?
Maybe a bit of pinot grigio – not too dry –
Romaine and a splash of Caesar, dotted
with croutons toasted in garlic.
Then, at the end, a square of dark chocolate
with a macadamia nut or two, - no, no,
peach cobbler baked in well-browned butter
bubbling inside.

Forget it. Don't mess with perfection!
Just the slab of salmon on a cedar plank, please.

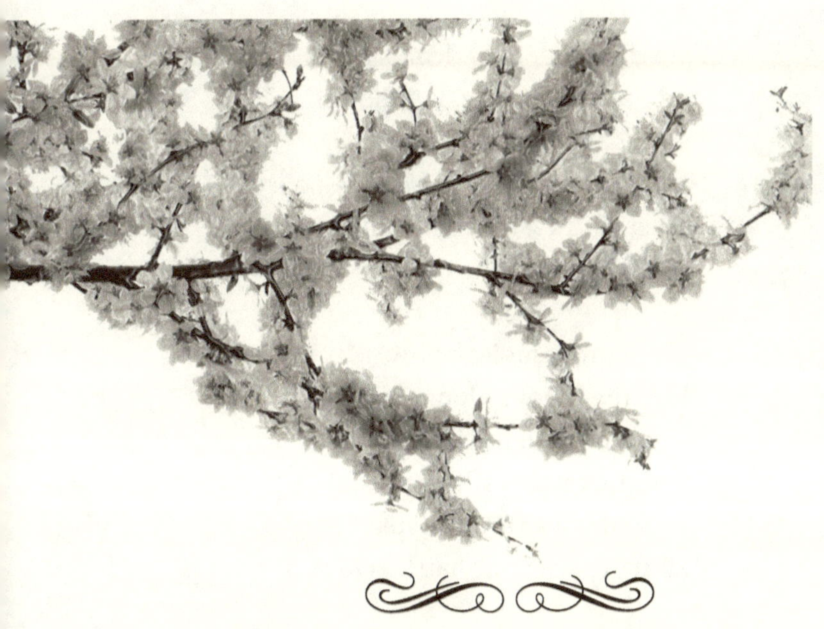

IN THE MUSEUM

DAVID BY MICHELANGELO

Your alabaster skin drinks me in
and I am lost in my own libido.
You have wrecked my heart
for any other perfection, your smooth curves
and sweet softness, I scarce can breathe
for the wanting of you.

I grow moist below
but must move along. I wish
you were in my bedroom
and not on this silly pedestal
with these silly people
waiting to see your hairless face.

Then I remember the reality
of your touch and temper,
the cold, hard, unrelenting truth of you,
the unmoving soul of you,
A statue that speaks not of love,
nor longing, nor life, but only beauty.

So I choose the flaws of a real life,
the frustrating, disappointing, ignorant,
yet warm and breathing truth of you.
I choose you.

DINNER WITH JUDY CHICAGO

I'd love to sit at Judy's table
eating a sumptuous dinner
with her best-dressed guests of note,
sitting side by side.

What would I, could I say to the thoughts
of those faces that make me feel
the otherness of being there?
Is there a fee to join this club?

What finery allows me to enter here?
Or is this an excess I'll never know?
Thoughts too high for contemplation
in my simple and poorly appointed life?

What is your point, Judy Chicago?
Help us solve the enigma.
No black, nor brown, nor unadorned beauty,
I can only guess at your puzzled message.

THE MERCHANTMEN
BY REMBRANDT

Menacing darkness foretells the evil sought,
the profit that spreads and infects.
Rapacious appetites for more and more.
The Corporate Cocks know no limit.

Money destroys and enslaves, but
the Corporate Cocks care not for those
who languish and die for their selfish desires.
Homelessness, starvation, disease and deep pain,
the uselessness and loss of spirit and soul.

The Corporate Cocks care not, nor will admit
there's no future for this assaulted earth.
They only pretend to save, as they suck another dollar
from the hellish fields and forests they have raped
and ravaged for yet another penny for their fortunes.

THE IRISES BY VAN GOGH

I have captured you forever
on a sweatshirt of mine.

It's my favorite, you know,
I wish you could see it and
feel it - it's so warm.
Ahhhh.

Yet with time, it has balled up,
become itchy and weary to wear.
Like everything else in life,
its usefulness dimmed and full of tears.

THE GARDENS OF MONET

I traveled to France to see in person the gardens
of renown, a poor imitation of his paintings.

But there is a hush there, a rustling that restores the eye.
If I squint a bit, I can see him

on the other side of the lake
painting, painting, always painting,

but I prefer not to cross the ocean again.

DANCING WITH DEGAS

I have studied ballet,
worn the tutu and toe shoes, pli-ed
and cracked my fingers into a curly pose,
squatted at the barre
in knee bends and arabesques.

I graduated out of sixth grade follies
to homecoming dances in the gym,
furtive glances from sweaty boys
and girls with jealous eyes, wearing
pink poodle skirts with pleats.

The Degas dancers are frozen forever,
locked into positions perfectly posed
and poised for the museum people
that parade through every day.
I'm glad not to be inside that eternity.

THE MELTING CLOCK
BY SALVADOR DALI

Ticking and tocking
Clicking and clocking

Time crushes and wears me down,
motivates and melts me,

Do it more and do it faster!
It slips and slithers in the heat.

Why must I go so fast?
It plays with my needs

like a cat with a ball of yarn.
Slow down, I say,
I am   m
        e
        l
         t
          i
           n
            g

PIETA

What kind of mother would let
her child die like that?

Her arms came too late to save.
She should have used her wiles
to stop this.

But mothers can't answer
for the deeds of their children.
The thing can't be undone in this life.

LA GUERNICA

How could war be beautiful?
an acquired art of injustice, pain and death?
bought unfairly at the price of horror to all?
Yet Picasso's anthem sings of beauty,
dancing on the wall to a macabre tune.

Do you hear the song?
Can you sing along?
Do you know at last
that wrong is wrong?

BLUE BOY AND PINKIE

Both hung above the dining room table
in my childhood home, masquerading
the beauty I would never achieve.
What was the meaning of their hanging there?
It was too subtle for me to grasp.

Am I just another child?
Another person struggling to be free,
aching to step out of the frame to know life?
to answer the questions that plague?
Who am I? And why?

I hang on the wall just like they,
condemned to ignorance and living that way.

ART OPENS LIFE

Art opens life so we can look at it
with another perspective,
The feeling on the page or canvass
reaches us in the core of our being
as nothing else can.

DEAD PEOPLE

REV. BUCHMUELLER

I was a snippet when first we met,
my hand warm in his wrinkled digits.

He said my birthmark was a gift
so God could find me in a crowd.

Sometimes we played the old organ.
On his lap I'd sit, my hands fiddling the keys.

The church, next to his modest house,
had thirteen steps to the sanctuary.

One Saturday we packed the steps with snow.
The whole neighborhood came with sleds and skates

and stuff and we were careful to take a turn
and brake before plowing into the street.

When Mother called, it was getting dark.
I was the last to leave. She put me into

an ice-filled bath. What were you thinking? she said.
You could get frost bite and lose your toes!

It was Sunday before she knew
about the iced-over thirteen steps

leading to the sanctuary for morning services.
I was just glad it was too cold for her to retrieve

a peach tree switch, frozen to a knobby baton,
and stripped of its leaves and love.

PROFESSOR ROBERT JAMES HASKINS, CONDUCTOR EXTRAORDINAIRE

An operatic role here and there,
a chance to shine, an oratorio,
a recital, or concert of high renown.
Why didn't I grasp his generosity?
He placed me where I could grow like a weed
in the skill and performance one would need
to be a singer of weight and substance.
Why was I so obtuse?
So unappreciative and unaware?

Some said he was a liar.
The big lie about his baseball career
too big to not believe.
But I knew him to be so big
he blanketed his stories
with a powerful personality
and the gifts of his huge heart.
As for his lies?
They were all true.

ZELDA

Heart to heart, she said, when she embraced me.
We were both big-breasted, she and I,
so the hug was something of a doozie.

My black priest was over six feet tall, imposing
as hell when you met her, first, last, and forever.

She was not shy about giving her love,
with a laugh or a tear, if your mood required,
she supplied a listening ear.

Our touch, boob to boob, and heart to heart,
was holy, she said, as she hugged me.

THE TRICK OR TREATERS

Halloween, of course, a scary day at best.
A dozen or so, ages nine to thirteen,
laughing and drooling with candy
as they left the market on Wilson Street.

A rival gang in a passing car - it makes me
weep to think of those sweet little Mama's boys,
Not yet callow or wise, but all of life ahead,
three soon dead, and four more wounded,

sweet licorice drooling and dripping
from a slack bloody mouth
and brains that pooled on the sidewalk.
They weren't from a rival gang at all.

Not the hated Crips, enemies and foes.
A mistaken identity, wrong place and time.
Just Halloween, of course,
a scary day at best.

MY PRIEST, GEORGE REGAS

He remembered my name
the second time we met.
He remembered my name
and he hugged me.

Never mind the money, thousands spent
and challenged by those who had druthers.
Never mind the anti-war protestors
who grieved the old timers.

Never mind the sadness he carried in his heart
for the thousands he'd loved and lost.
He made my heart bigger. He changed me
and grew me into the person I am today.

I often fell asleep in the choir loft
as he whispered the good thoughts of the day.
I'd wake with a start when he thundered,
shaking me to my withers to be better,

to be something, to be someone that mattered.
His love, so wide, so deep, guided and prodded me
to greater deeds. "God is in the work", he'd say and
there I found the love I'd lost so many years ago.

MY GRANDFATHER, THE RENAISSANCE MAN

A man for all seasons, was it required in those days?
Young years in a sod hut, carved in a west Kansas hill,
where Indians watched his new bride cook.
He deemed it unsafe.

He ran in the Oklahoma land run, the small plot was
to be nurtured and tended but he preferred
to ride by horse to teach English and Math,
lest farmers be cheated at the mill.

He bought a general store and built a home.
Three of eight children were birthed, but then,
the oil companies came to Oklahoma in a rush,
derricks were needed and such.

But there was no music on a Saturday night,
so he made fiddles, one for each child,
and rocking chairs too, for grandchildren who came in time,
after the load of a boxcar of peaches was sold,

fanned and canned by someone, somewhere,
and then, it was time, time to play checkers,
and to reflect on the legacy of those children.
And life was safe enough.

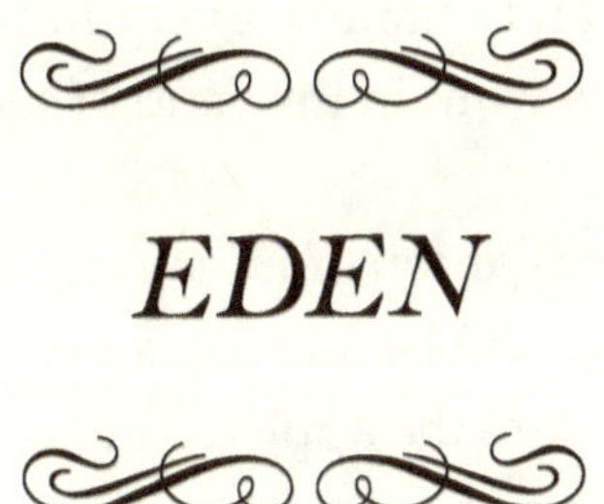

EDEN

EDEN

We've been living in Eden since Adam's day,
but the bouncer has come to oust us.
The apples have boosted our health and wellbeing,
but we've lost the privilege of our greed.

Our forefathers knew, plant only what you need,
and let the labored land rest. We laughed at warnings
and warmings, of fires and floods, but now
we're in the sixth extinction, a noxious screed.

Many have gone by already, plants and animals, birds of the air,
fish of the seas, we have chosen money and war over these.
"Profit is king and winning, everything. We will take
what we want in this land of the free."

Now our garden of Eden is fading fast.
Our story will be told to an empty earth.
We are the apple-eaters, and
Johnny will come no more.

TIME

Just another dimension
like Albert Einstein said?
Does it collapse to a line
in an infinity that spreads
out and out and out some more?
until our remembering dies
and we must come again?

and again. That's why, perhaps,
we can't learn a thing or two.
We must do it over and over.
Most of the time, the earth recovers,
And we never remember her pain.

But when there are too many wounds
and too many wounders to wound again
with slashes of coal-hungry diggers
and derricks of height, and malls,
and fashion, and houses with heat,
and gas-guzzling cars, and poor people strive
to stay alive, with mouths to feed,
and don't forget me, I need to eat.
but the moneyed monsters
never have enough.

NEVER ENOUGH

I could go into my closet and get dressed a hundred times.
Never mind I bought everything second hand,
I still have more than enough.
So what is enough? If everyone in the world
had just enough and no more, could we
survive another hour, a day, a year – or even a forever?
Would our Mother Earth be OK with that?

WAR AND PEACE

I dreamt of a scene in Tolstoy,
when the prince was wounded in battle.
His horse reared up and he saw in the sky
a joy-filled scene from the day before.
Soldiers running to the edge of a river
to play and bathe and laugh with the wetness,
and with the belief they would never die.

The two scenes were juxtaposed
one upon the other, and I saw for myself
the contrast of life and death.
We love life's beauty, but it's not enough.
Only evil, disease, cruelty and pain
teach us to value the good, the kind, and the sane.

War and peace – a contradiction and a conundrum,
necessary evils for the ages.

MY LITTLE GARDEN

I wish I could bind up the earth, apply
healing ointment on her slashes and cuts.
I want to convince the Corporate Cocks
they will doom us all with their gluttony.

I visit the oil fields,
the forests logged away.
I smell the poisoned air
and hear the brackish waters.

I was raised in a class that doesn't care,
as long as we have our nighttime toddy,
and a vacation on the beach somewhere.
We already joined the Sierra Club.

So I water my little garden
though I haven't a green thumb.
I couldn't grow something if my life
depended on it. Except…
it does – perhaps it does.
It really does.

TONGLEN

Breathe in, breathe out
Breathe in, breathe out
Inhale the ills of the world
trillions as they are,
injustice, hatred,
cruelty, ignorance,
folly and greed.
It's all there – in the tip
of the iceberg to come.

Breathe in, breathe out
Breathe in, breathe out
Exhale what goodness you can,
a tiny bit, a bud about to be,
a mouse, a moose, a rabbit turned loose
a second chance to be alive,
a mountain, a lake, for goodness' sake,
beauty to the love-seeking eye.

You can be the difference, exhale
and exhale again, all your love for all you see,
and gratitude for the things that be.

COMPASSION

Compassion is too big for me.
It looms and crashes willy-nilly
across the highways and byways of life.
I hear of it almost every day.

Someone gave a kidney, another the heart itself,
an elephant carried a lion cub to the waterhole,
a mother lifted a car to set her baby free,
and folks funded a funeral on Go Fund Me.

Compassion runs rampant throughout the world,
in every clime and culture. So why do we even bother
with life's opposite – the selfish, greedy kind?
We can never do enough, have enough.

Compassion. A thing of beauty indeed, but
it's so much easier to love.

WHAT IF?

What if I could snap my fingers
And make it all OK?

What if I could turn back time
to learn the earth was enough for all, after all?
before the robber barons and corporate cocks
stripped and stole Gaia's heart and soul?

What if I could stop the mining, save the trees,
waste no water, power with the tides, the sun and wind?
What if I could make everything simple, but equal -
good food, good water, and a good home for all?

Is it too much to ask? Too much of a burden?
To be the same on a perishing plant?
Or is the end of all things what we truly want
and what we are willing to bear?

HOPE

HOPE

There are pieces I cannot bare to share.
I am not only naked, but skinless,
and so tender I am cut to the bone,
but nevertheless, I find hope.

When one yields to the future.
a future uncertain, perhaps hurtful,
when one repairs, yet surrenders all,
nevertheless, one finds hope.

We have no way of our own,
no skill or access to save it all.
Only in the awareness of the now
can we find gratitude and joy

Perhaps, we learn to live and love,
and perhaps, to wake in freedom.
Then, and then, nevertheless,
we find hope.

THOUGHTS IN BRIEF

From Thich Nhat Hanh
No mud, no lotus

From Ann Spier
The world is a muddy place.

A Good Friend
He/she/it never tells me what to do,
but stands by to comfort
when I've made a bad decision.

Nevertheless
No matter how often I yell at you
And blame you for my erring ways,
I don't believe.
No way, no how,
it's all preposterous,
a crutch,
a senseless escape for weaklings.
Nevertheless, God,
help me thou my unbelief.

A CONVERSATION WITH SOME ONE NOT ALL THERE

Are you a God?
Or are you The God?
Or one of many?
Whatever.
All I want to say is
Thank you.

For the stars, the trees, the mountains,
for water and clean air, for all I see and more,
I can't even remember everything I'm grateful for.
As I walk down the street, I find more stuff – flowers,
and weeds, and every other walking person and oh!
I forgot the animals, the rhinos and baboons,
elephants and lions, and all the rest in the zoo,
and my puppies! But most of all,
I'm grateful for our time together,
when we sit in my chair and talk, you and I.

I've finally learned to listen, at least for a second or two,
because the best things come when I'm near you,
and I hear you.

Are you a god or are you The God?
Whatever. I don't need to know.
But sometimes, I wonder,
are you the better part of myself?

THE NORFOLK PINE

The wind comes from the north.
Hard on, it blows, the fronds
in a dance to the death, it seems,
swaying and flaying as the wind plays
its tunes on tireless branches.

Even the birds stay home
when the wind groans and grimaces.
What masseuse pulls and pushes the trunk
in this aerobic exercise of back bends?

The squirrels hide now, no music
chastens and chases them,
hopping briskly, bragging, they leap
to the orange tree yonder.

The Pine and I have grown old together,
from the two sides of my sliding door.
In rain-tossed storms and peaceful heat,
I've watched and suffered with my friend.

In stillness and silence, she stands on guard,
watching me even as I watch her.
A sort of family, we breathe
for a sick earth as we wait, listening.

SENTIENT BEINGS

Do you suppose they are jealous of the way
we walk on two legs? Do they judge us for eating them up?
Or perhaps they wish only for a better recipe?

My dog Shakespeare, I'm sure, wants a golden thread
to tie us two. He's a better empath than I.
Is he smarter? Perhaps. His nose certainly is, and maybe
his ears as well. But in some things, he's in kindergarten still.

It's all that napping, I am sure, that holds him back
from high school. If only he could read while he waits
for me, then give a book report as we walk the streets.
I should love to share my thoughts with him.

We could discuss the news of the trees and that blade of grass
that smells of Roxie's pee and listen for the black pit bull
that barks from the garage next door.
My dog barks when we see him waiting on the porch.

NAMASTE

My spirit greets your spirit
Can you hear them loving each other?
Do you think they are friends,
though we've never met before?

We are the same, you and I,
though you weave on a loom day by day
making a serape for tourists like me.
You may worry to have enough to eat today,
or a place to feel safe today.
Sometimes you may feel yourself lucky
to live in nature, day by day,
weaving, weaving.

Namaste.
Do you know our spirits
are one and the same?
Do you know they joyfully recognize
their love for one other
whether we know it or not?
Day by day.

LOVE LANGUAGES

How do I love thee?
Let me count the ways.

You get my choir music lest I have to climb the stairs.
You wash up after dinner, cleaning up the spills,
scarcely minding you made them to begin with.

At the first sound of danger,
your head snaps to mine.
Is she alright, your frantic eyes say.
Am I needed? Are you OK?

May I open a jar, close a door,
carry the weight, chase away evil,
a zipper, a button, a toenail, a belt,
brush some hair, reach to high places,
or the computer, perhaps,
needs a change of pace?

As for me,
I play golf.

Concept from Gary Chapman's book The Five Love Languages

ONE-ING

If I sit here long enough
and if I wait in silence
with breath abated and still,
maybe you will come.

They say mindfulness is the way
to learn of yourself
and to find the peace that knows
all is well.

But behind this mess call life,
the facts refuse to move
and I tumble about in the turbulent
waves of a scourging river, tossing

my limbs akimbo, face asunder,
I fight for breath, for purchase
of a branch or something
to stop the fall of living.

In pain and anguish, in regret and sadness,
I tumble about in the water.
my screams drowned by the smash and
crash of river against the rocks of life.

It gulps me under and I shriek,
for if I go down, I'll not come up.
It is my wish perhaps– to drown,
to stay down in the depths of my anguish.

Yet my comeuppance comes
as a moment of acceptance
reposes my soul and I know
I can catch a breath.

The water fills and freshens,
no longer my foe, I take it in
like the air I breathe,
one and the same.

It is the One-ing that comes.
I sit in stillness
and in profound silence.
I open my mind and soul.
I listen.
I find all is well,
All that is, is well.
And all will be well.

THE OLD HYMN

Melt me, mold me,
Fill me, use me
That's what the old hymn says.

Some of the melting I've done
was entirely my own fault.
It hurt a lot, nonetheless, too late
to melt and mend my erring ways.

As for molding, it's a lifetime journey.
Sometimes I go backwards a bit
to mold in a false and feckless shape.
But when I wake, I am "woke" to it all.

Fill me doesn't start until I'm emptied,
until I've surrendered all.
Then it feels good, like molten gold and joy.
I have found my purpose and my way.

As for the last –
Use me -
I should be so lucky.

THE MONKEY MIND

In the silence
In the stillness
I wait

I wonder if David remembered to turn off the heat last night. Our gas bill is ridiculous these days. In fact I wonder if he remembered to pay the bill. Of course, there's no penalty if you are late. It's not like the ridiculous fines we get on credit cards. Why can't we get caught up? Why…

In the silence
In the stillness
I wait

This is ridiculous. Why can't I find the zone today? My mind just won't go there. Maybe I should get up and start doing all the stuff I need to do. No, Martin Luther said it was important to pray even more when you had a lot to do. But this isn't praying. This is so much harder. I've been practicing for… let's see 50- no, 54 years in March. Wow, I should celebrate! Oh hush! Of all the things to be proud of. There goes my ego again. Shit!

In the silence
In the stillness
I wait

I haven't written a poem in two months. Maybe there's something
wrong with me. I really don't have any talent. Who do I think I
am – faking a literary life? No one would miss it if I never wrote
another word. It's all junk anyway. Although I do sometimes get
a good idea when I'm meditating. If I could quiet this monkey
mind, I could focus. No, not focus. I just want to get in the zone.
I haven't had a good session in quite a while. All this itching
distracts me.

In the silence
In the stillness
I wait.

See, I can't even sit still. This is a waste of time. I should just give
up. I am a farce, a fake.

Wait, wait, there it is,
ahhhh
No, now it's gone.
But I'm closer,
I feel the quietude.
The hush of another
The Oneness
Silence
Stillness
zzzzzz

I AM THANKFUL

First, for the earth, and second, for art,
not of the workaday world,
but humankind's best
and most thoughtful creations.

And most, for ordinary things,
family, dogs, children, good food,
for bravery, kindness, and good deeds.

Yes, for good deeds, best of all.
I am thankful for those who help others.

And finally, I am thankful for the love of God –
not so much that God loves me –
which is a given because I live –
but because I love God in spite of
not having the faintest idea
who or what God is.

I SIT WITH ANGELS

Dedicated to the Women of Spirit

Before they leave, they put
a smile on my soul

They don't always come,
Perhaps I have offended or maybe
it's the other way 'round
I just don't hear them that day.

Angels don't always sing, you know.
unless you are quiet from head to toe,
the kind of quiet that finds you empty
of anger and fear.

There has to be a place,
you see, for the angels to send
their words, for the angels
simply to be.

I sit with angels.
How do I know?

Before they leave, they put
a smile on my soul.

THE WISDOM WELL

Take a drink at the wisdom well.
Its waters will do you good.
Its waters are chaste and pure.
You'll crave no other food.

A bit of sitting gives your soul a chance
to grow and flourish, to clear its eyes.
Take a sip of forgiving, then
let it go like a freed bird.

Pray for a loved one, visit someone lonely.
Your presence is more powerful than you know.
Pay a compliment, deserved or not,
and the smile you see will grow,

and be remembered, like your presence in the dark
and despair of some other's nightmare.
So it is, you give, and give again, and even
if you have naught to give, it's the thought that heals.

The little deeds become love purified,
a love chastened in joy, a love
that multiplies and magnifies
from one to another, contagious, you know.

Take a drink at the wisdom well,
Sit, forgive, give and pray,
Visit, praise, and let it go,
It's easier to love that way.

INVITATION TO THE DANCE

Join in the dance,
Eat the feast of life.
Let your sorrows fly.
Deny the beast of selfhood and lie,
lie, lie if you have to,
to lift your voice in song.

The birds know the words.
You can start with imitation.
Then your heart will find a road
to the well-traveled way you once knew
and walked for many a day –
the road of peace, of praise, of joy.

Join in the dance,
Won't you?

PEACH COBBLER

Preheat oven to 425 degrees

One stick of (salted) butter
One cup of flour
One cup on sugar
One cup of milk
One tsp. of baking powder
Two cups of sliced ripe peaches

Put the butter in a baking dish (9x12)
and place in oven for 20-30 minutes.
This is the most important part. The
butter must be melted, bubbling and
sizzling and BROWN.

Add the next four ingredients without stirring,
then add peaches throughout dish, but again,
without stirring too much.

Bake 25-30 minutes at 425 degrees
until tooth pick comes out clean.
Serve with vanilla ice cream (or not).
Mange!